AF802999

BOOK-ONE

THREE R's

for

SNARE DRUM

Reading - Rhythms - Rudiments

by

ACTON E. OSTLING

Alfred

FOREWORD

This book is designed to supply supplementary material for snare drum students to be used after, or in conjunction with, any Beginner's method—to aid in developing reading ability, and the applying of rudiments as used in band and orchestra playing.

Note the following:

1. The exercises are in progressive form, starting with very simple fundamentals.
2. At least one NEW point is introduced on each page. No rhythm pattern, expression mark, rudiment, or any fundamental is used in any exercise until it has been introduced in one of the "boxes" at top of pages.
3. The student should be sure of the meaning of each NEW point before proceeding with exercises on any page.
4. Short preparatory exercises precede the regular material on each page. Drill these as needed.
5. In addition to the exercise material, each page has an excerpt from standard band literature, showing how the fundamental introduced on that page is used in an actual number.
6. As most drum music is written with single notes only (no rudiments) many of the exercises in this book are written likewise. Suggestions for applying rudiments to rhythm patterns are given as the various rudiments are introduced. Instructors who prefer single sticking, or who have a definite system of applying rudiments may disregard these.
7. Exercises may be taken at any speed. Original tempo markings are used for the standard excerpts.
8. All material is numbered each 4 measures for easy reference in class lessons.
9. The 38 NEW points covered in Book One are as follows (in order of introducing):

1. 4/4
2. ♩
3. 𝄽
4. C
5. 𝄆 𝄇
6. 3/4
7. 𝄎
8. ♫
9. 2/4
10. ♪
11. 𝄾
12. f
13. p
14. 𝄎 | 𝄎 | 𝄎 |
15. Flam
16. mf
17. ♩̸ = ♫
18. 1. :‖ 2. ‖
19. >
20. Roll
21. Tie
22. 𝄻
23. 3
24. Substituting rudiments for rhythms.
25. 5 Stroke Roll
26. ♪♬
27. ♬♪
28. 𝅘𝅥𝅯𝅘𝅥𝅯𝅘𝅥𝅯𝅘𝅥𝅯
29. Single Paradiddle
30. 𝅗𝅥
31. 𝄼
32. 𝅗𝅥.
33. 6/8-Slow
34. 6/8-Fast
35. Flam Accent No. I
36. Flam Accent No. II
37. Substituting Flam Accents for rhythms.
38. 9 Stroke Roll

Opening and Closing Drum Rudiments

Drum students should practice "opening and closing" the various drum rudiments, as follows:

Start any rudiment at a very slow speed (open); gradually speed it up, notes getting nearer together (closer) until fastest speed is reached (closed); then reverse the procedure, gradually getting slower (more open) until back at starting speed.

This "opening and closing" is required at all drum contests, and is excellent practice for any drummer.

The exercises in this book (and Book Two which follows) supply a considerable amount of varied reading material for the drum student. With careful practice and close attention to details, the student who completes—and understands—this material should be well along toward being a proficient reader of Snare Drum music.

TO THE STUDENT

1. Be sure that you understand the meaning of each NEW fundamental.
2. Carefully watch every mark in each exercise (especially from page 10 on).
3. Keep steady rhythm (count aloud, or beat foot, as instructed).
4. Perfect each exercise before going to the next.

NEW:= 1 2 3

Preparation

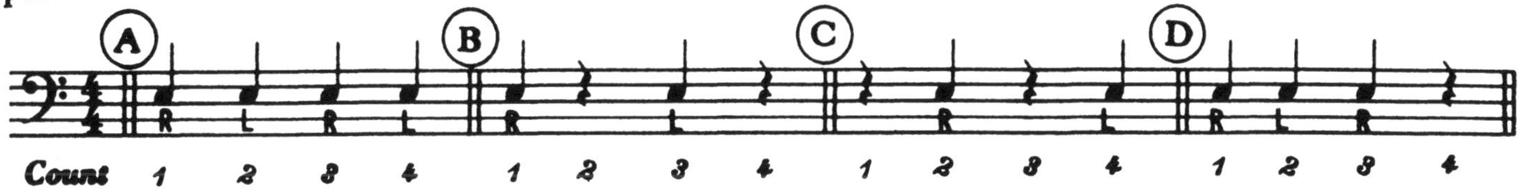

Single strokes—hand to hand.

1

2

3

4

Excerpt from "If I Were King" Overture

Moderato (*medium tempo*) A. ADAM

5

NEW:= 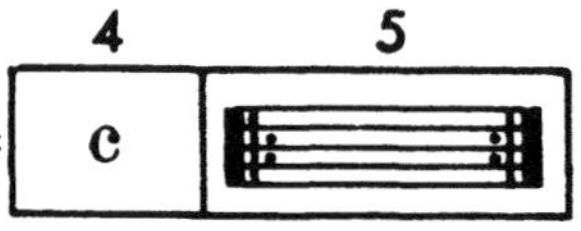

Preparation

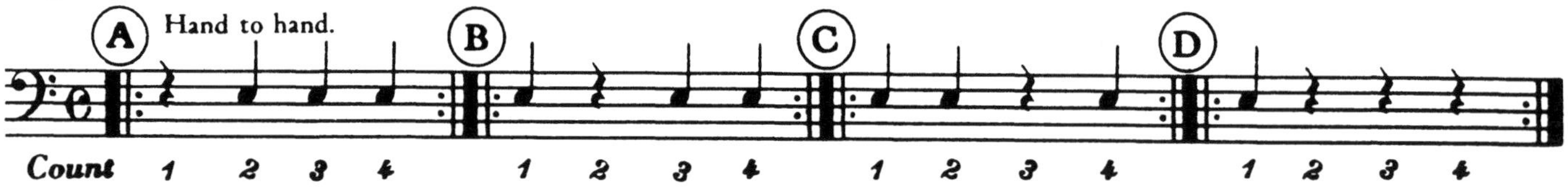

Excerpt from "Overture Militaire"

Allegro (*quick, lively*)

JOSEPH SKORNICKA

6

NEW:= 3/4

Preparation

Excerpt from "Egmont"

LUDVIG VAN BEETHOVEN

NEW:= 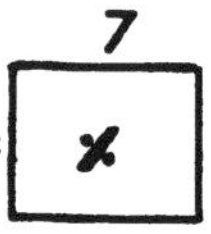

Preparation

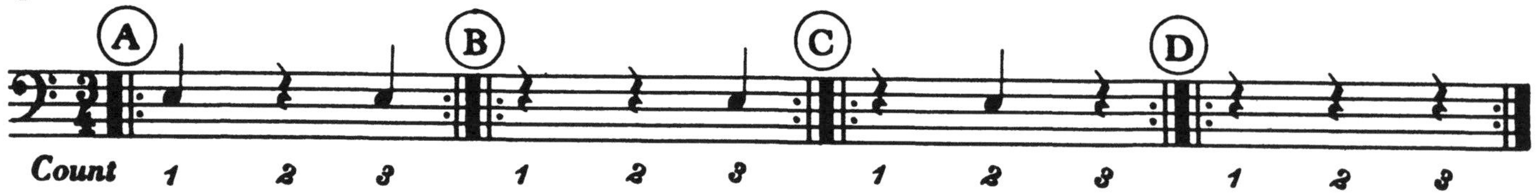

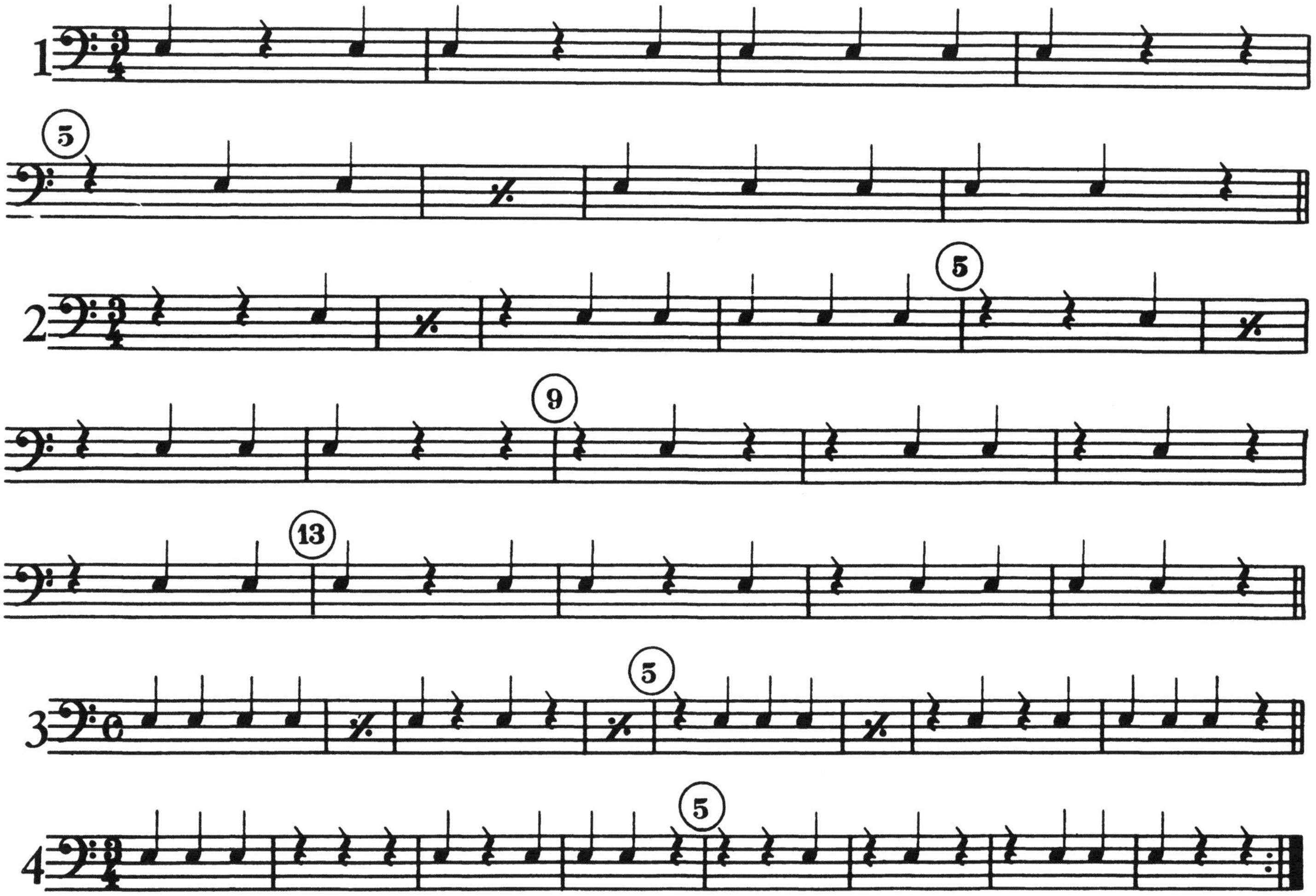

Excerpt from "Blue Danube" Waltz

JOHANN STRAUSS

NEW:= 

Preparation

Slow March

Maestoso (*majestically*)

NEW: = 9 [2/4]

Preparation

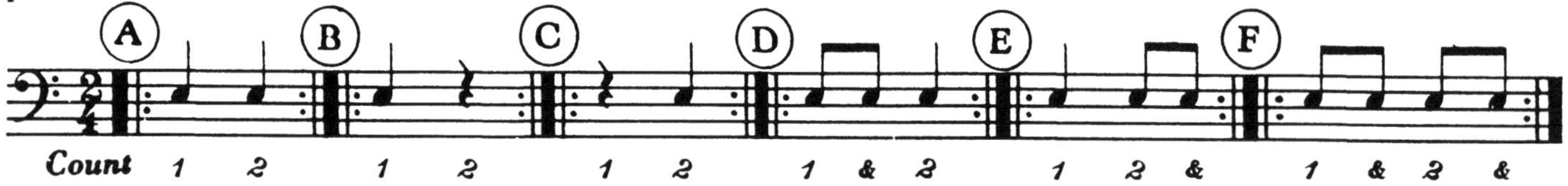

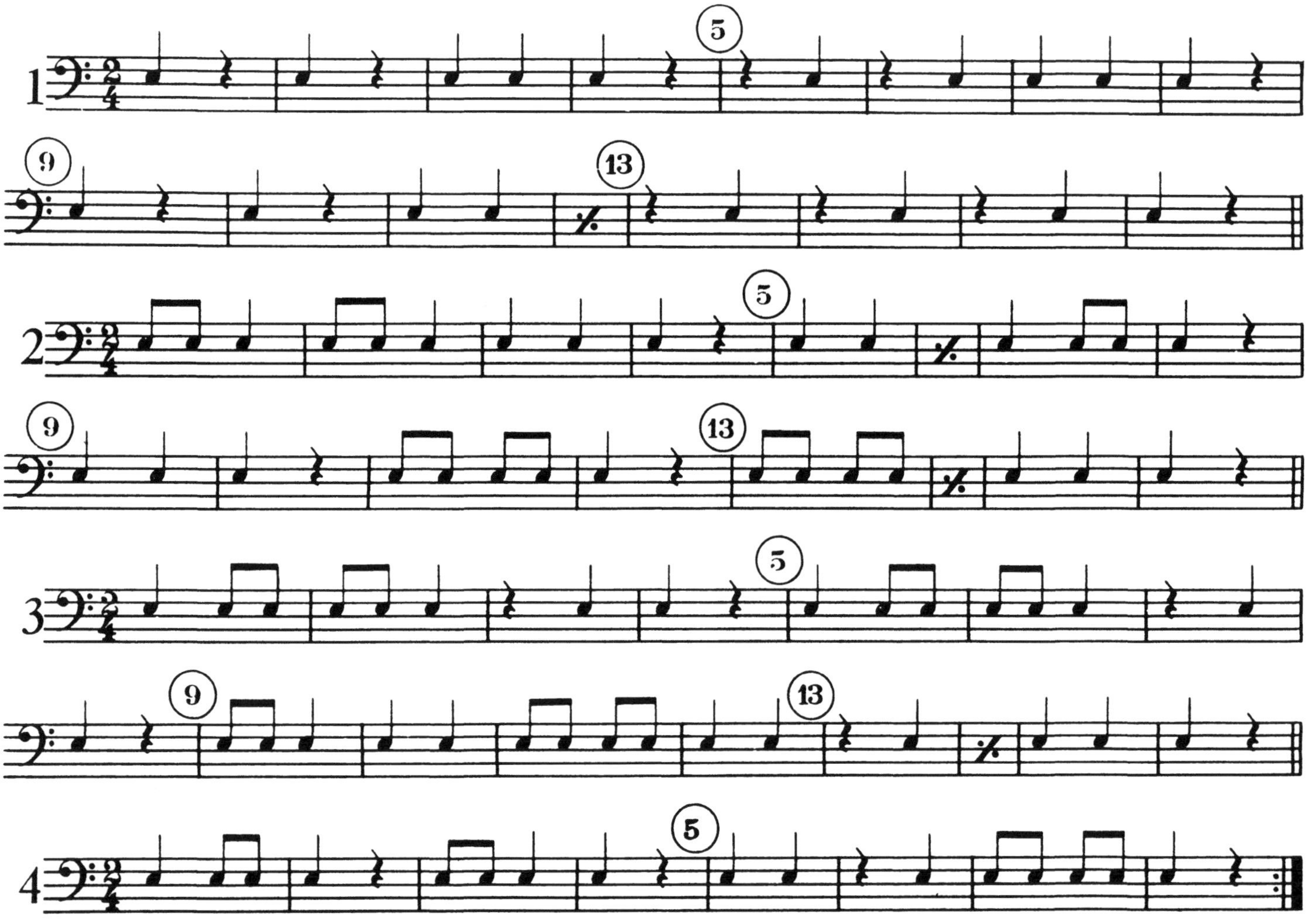

Excerpt from "Poet and Peasant" Overture

VON SUPPE

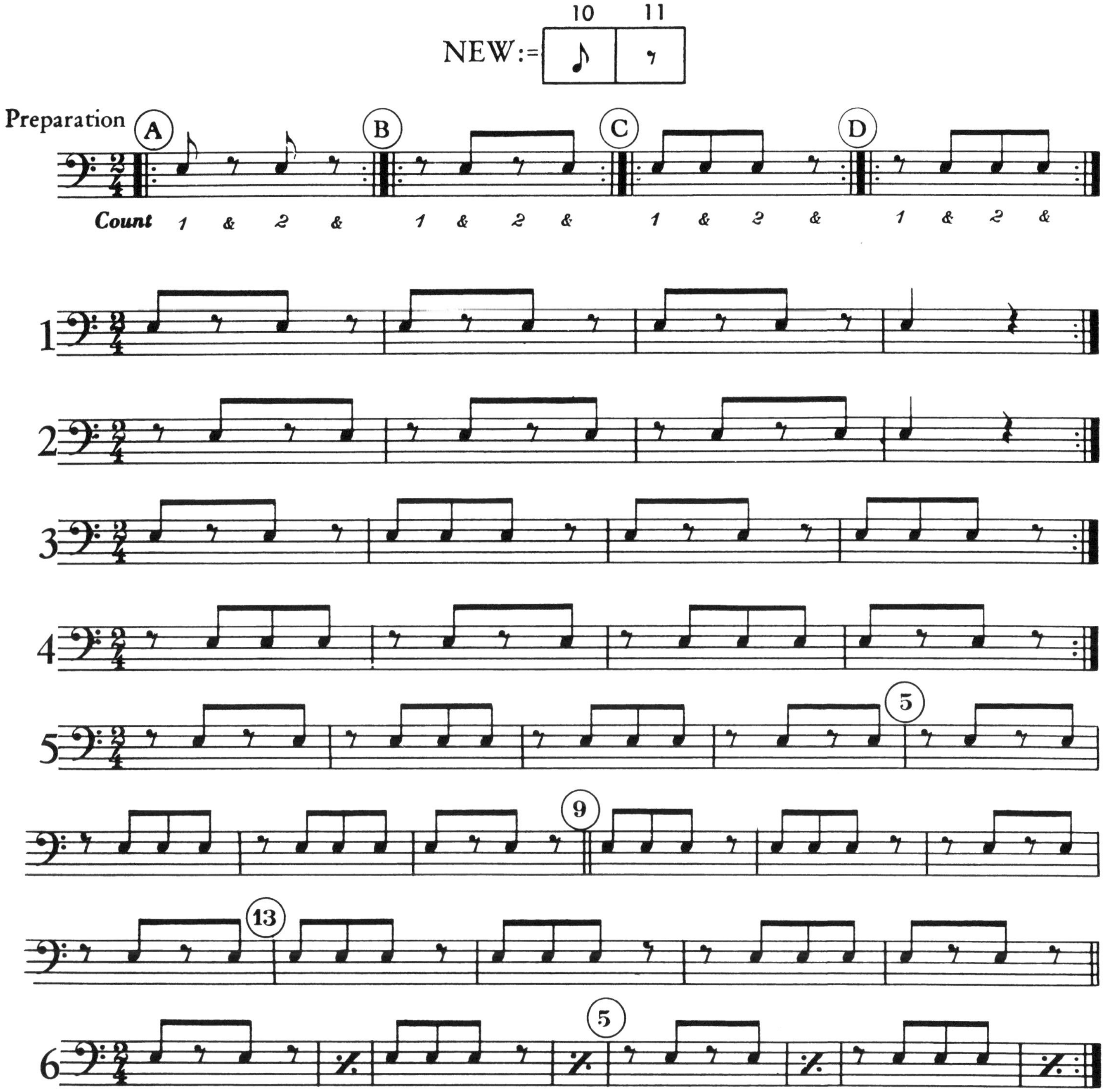

Excerpt from "Raymond" Overture

A. THOMAS

Allegro con moto

NEW:=	12	13
	f	*p*

Preparation

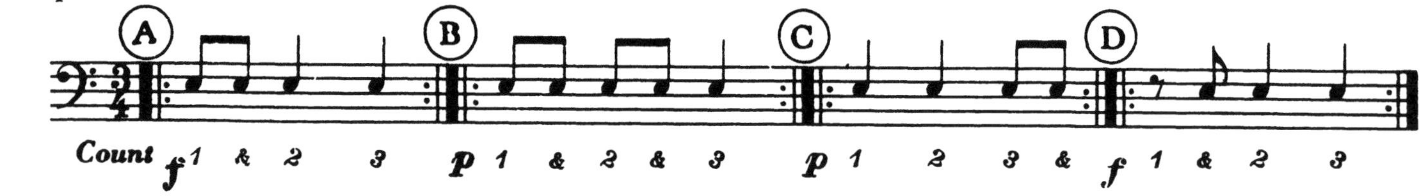

Watch marks of expression in all exercises from here on.

Grand March

Grandioso (*pompous, majestic*)

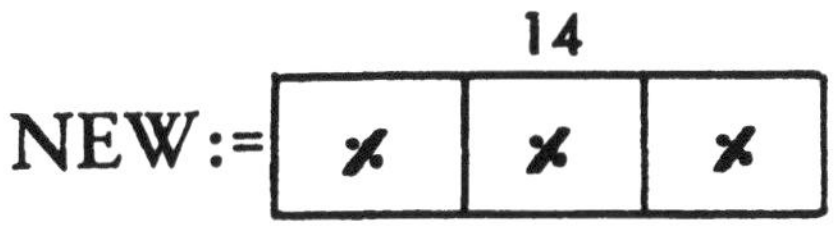

Preparation

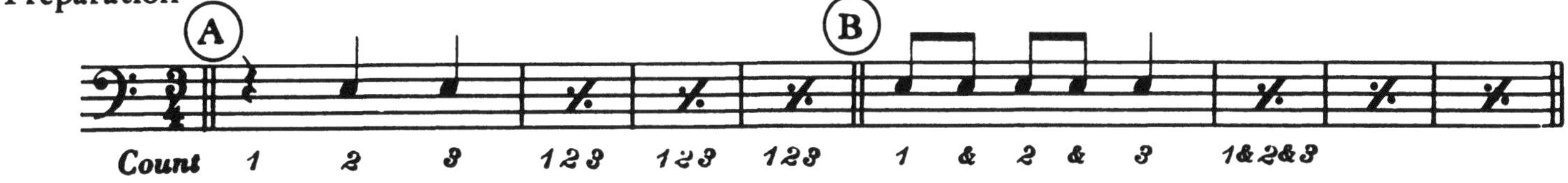

Second Strain "The Post Quartermaster" March

Tempo di Marcia (*in march time*)

LOUIS SAVERINO

15

Note:—F=R H. Flam. (L R)

(F)=L H. Flam (R L)

NEW:= **Flam:**

Note: Open and close flams daily

Preparation

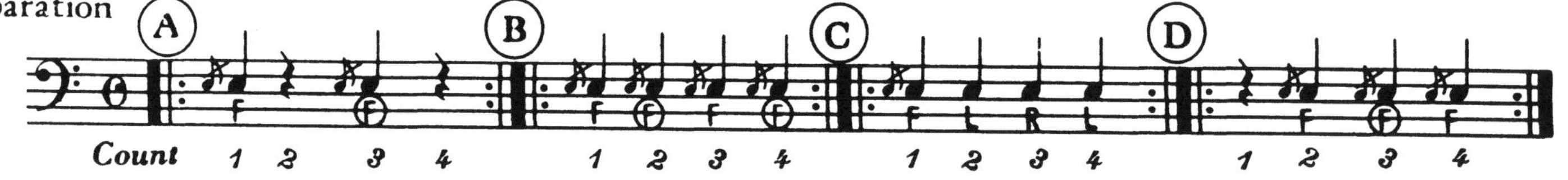

Excerpt from "Gypsy Princess" Overture

PAUL YODER

NEW:= 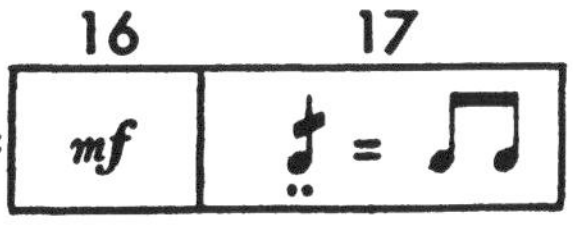

Note: Practice single strokes and flams in three volumes. *p*, *mf*, *f*

Preparation

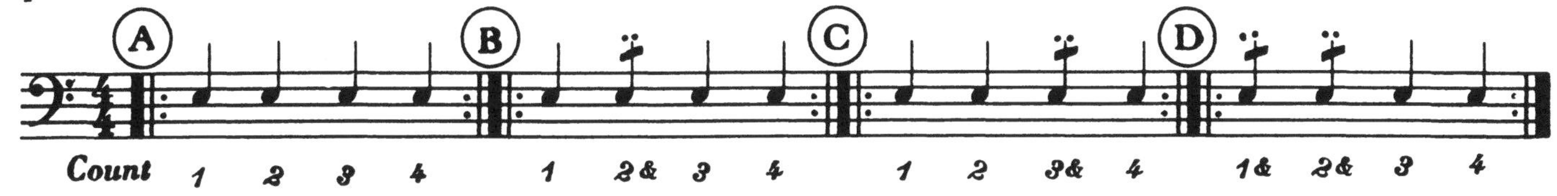

Excerpt from "Overture Militaire"

JOSEPH SKORNICKA

Maestoso

18
NEW:=
Preparation
A
1
2
mf
5
9
f
13
17
21
p
1
2
3
4

19
NEW: = >

Note: Watch all accents carefully—they are very important for drummers as the percussion section is so often used to reinforce accents by the full band or orchestra.

Preparation

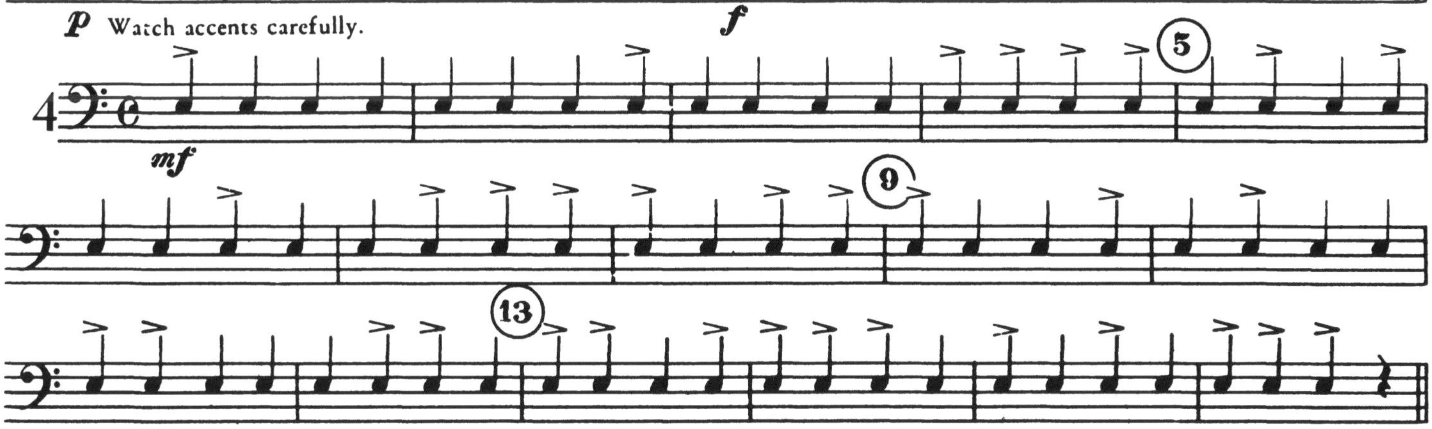

Mexican Clapping Song

NEW:= 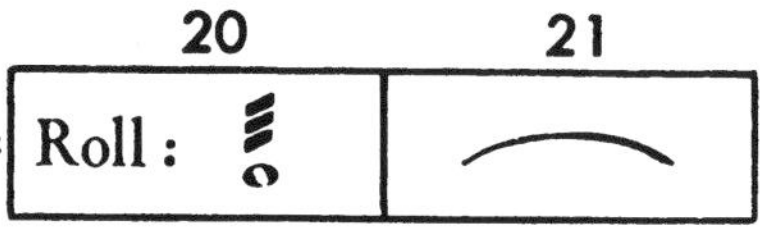

Note: (a) Open and close the long roll daily.
(b) Practice the closed roll in three volumes. *p*, *mf*, *f*

Preparation

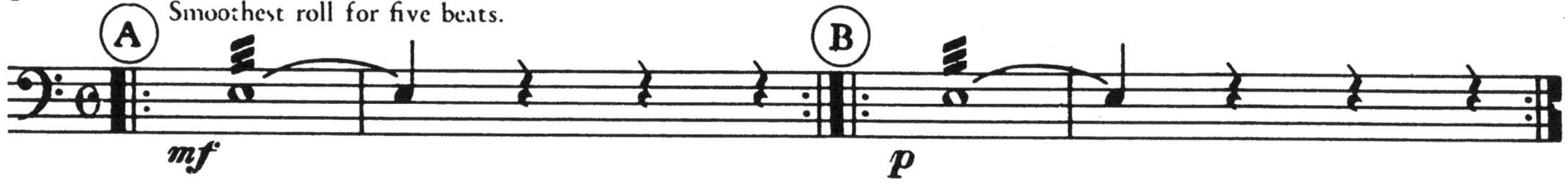

Excerpt from "Poet and Peasant" Overture

VON SUPPE

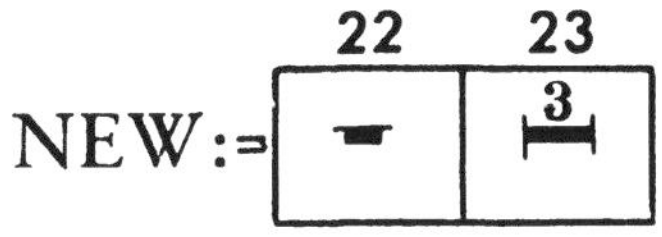

Preparation

Introduction "Light Cavalry" Overture

Maestoso

VON SUPPE

NEW:= Substituting Rudiments for Rhythms

Some drum parts have the rudiments clearly indicated, leaving no doubt as to how they should be played. However, many arrangers score the drum parts with rhythms only, leaving it to the individual drummer to apply rudiments. What rudiments to apply, and when to apply them depends on the type of music, the wishes of the director, and experience of the drummer. Single sticking is usually preferred in soft strains, light delicate passages, and where the tempo is very fast. However, in many places, the application of rudiments gives a distinctly "drummistic" effect which cannot be obtained with single sticking. Suggestions for applying the various rudiments will be given as they are introduced.

Preparation

As written

As played

Substitute hand to hand flams for all notes in the following exercises.

March Trio

Waltz

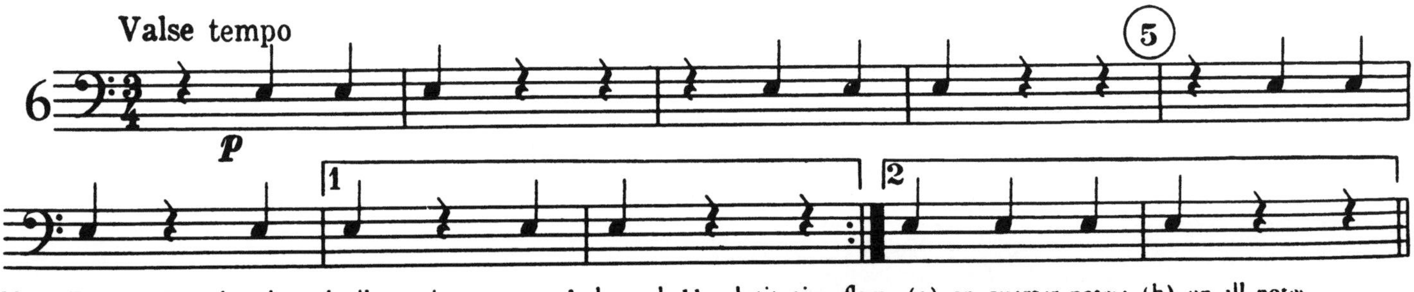

Note: For practice, play through all exercises on pages 3 through 11 substituting flams (a) on quarter notes; (b) on all notes

25

NEW: = 5 Stroke Roll :

Preparation

Note: Open and close 5 stroke rolls daily.

The notation for the 5 stroke roll, and for the 7 stroke roll is the same. The type of roll to play depends on the ability of the student, and the speed of the number. If the student is able to play 7's, they may be substituted for any roll notated or at the discretion of the instructor (7 stroke rolls are not introduced in this series until Book Two.)

26

NEW:= 

Preparation

Excerpt from "Coronation March" from "The Prophet"

Maestoso

G. MEYERBEER

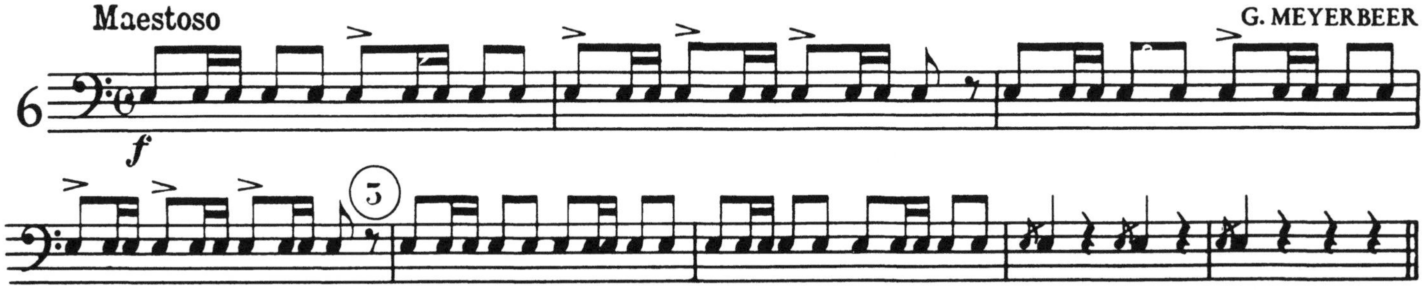

27

NEW:= 

Preparation

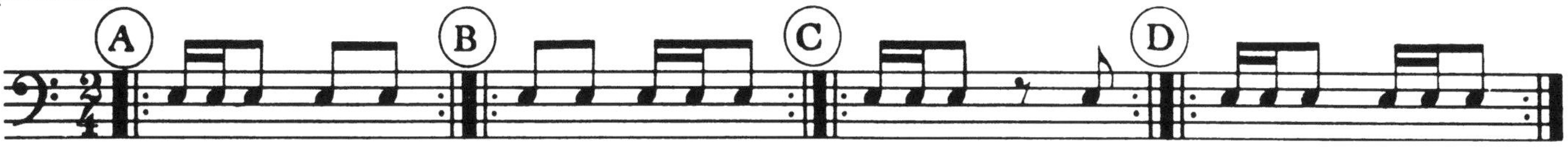

Count 1 a & 2 & 1 & 2 a & 1 a & 2 & 1 a & 2 a &

First Strain "The Leatherneck" March

LOUIS SAVERINO

March tempo

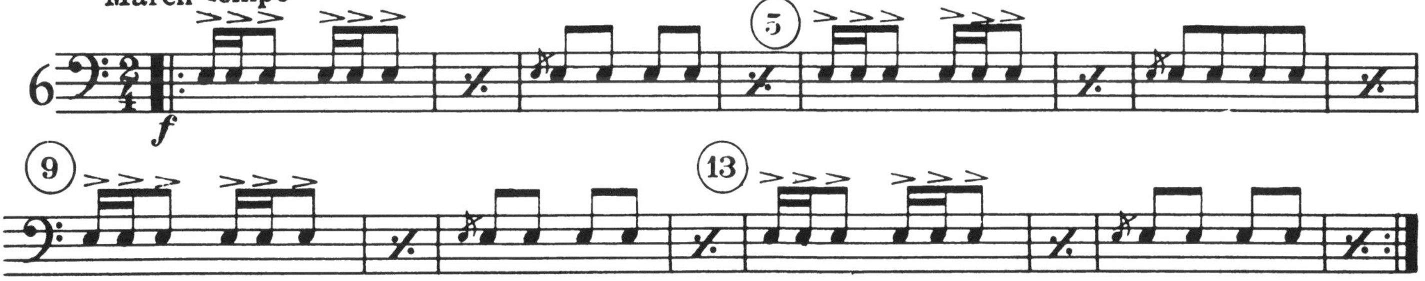

NEW:= 

Preparation

Parade of the Marionettes

S. J. MUSTOL

NEW:= Single Paradiddle : 

General rule: When two or more groups of sixteenth notes come in succession, they MAY be played as paradiddles.

Preparation

Note: Open and close the single paradiddle daily.

Excerpt from "Scenes Pittoresques"

J MASSENET

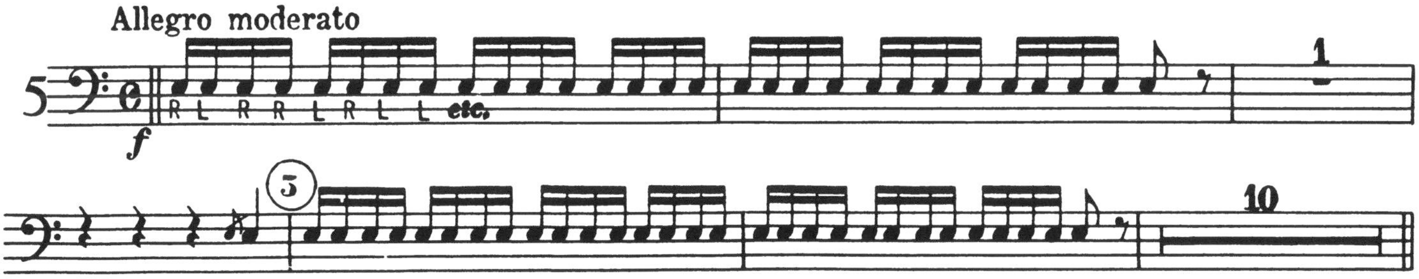

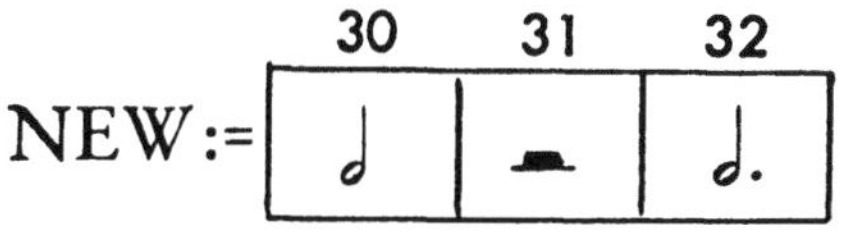

Preparation

Excerpt from Overture "Eroica"

JOSEPH SKORNICKA

33

NEW:= 6/8 — Slow

Excerpt from Overture "Semiramide"

G. ROSSINI

34

NEW: 6/8 — Fast

Excerpt from "Men of Action" March

LOUIS SAVERINO

35

NEW:= Flam Accent No. I

Open close Flam Accents No. 1 daily.

Preparation

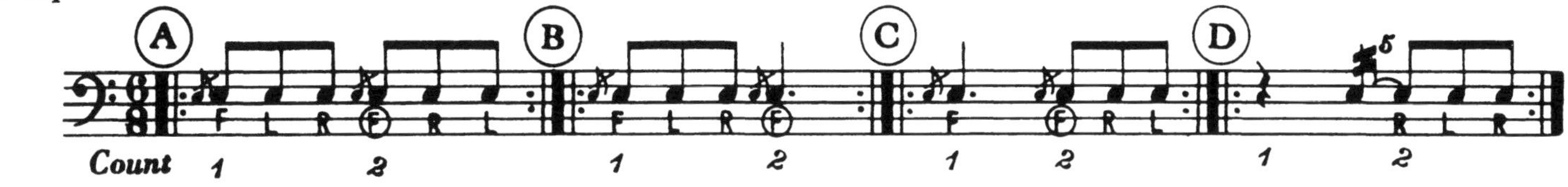

Excerpt from "Semper Fidelis" March

JOHN PHILIP SOUSA

The sticking of Flam Accent No 1 (F-L-R or (F)-R-L) may be applied advantageously, at times, to NEW patterns No 26 and 27, as follows: F L R or (F) R L, F L R or (F) R L. For practice, play the exercises on pages 20 and 21, applying this sticking to these patterns

NEW: = Flam Accent No. II

Open and close Flam Accents No 2 daily

Preparation

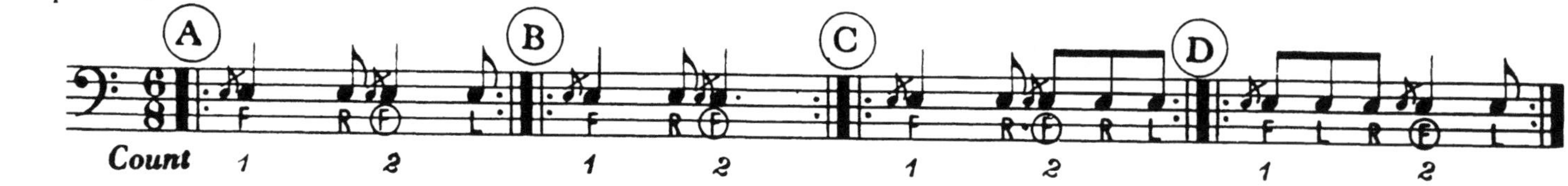

Excerpt from "Our Regiment" March

VAN DYCK

The sticking of Flam Accent No. II (F-R or F-L) may be applied to any group of two eighth notes, as follows: F R or F L. For practice, play through previous exercises, applying this sticking to ad lib (This is taken up further under Flam Taps in Book Two.)

NEW: = Substituting Flam Accents for Rhythm Patterns

The drum parts of six-eight marches are much more effective when Flam Accents are substituted as indicated here

Preparation

As written

As played

Substitute Flams and Flam Accents in the following exercises

Second Strain "Guardsmen" March

WALTER DESMOND

38

NEW: = 9 Stroke Roll

Preparation

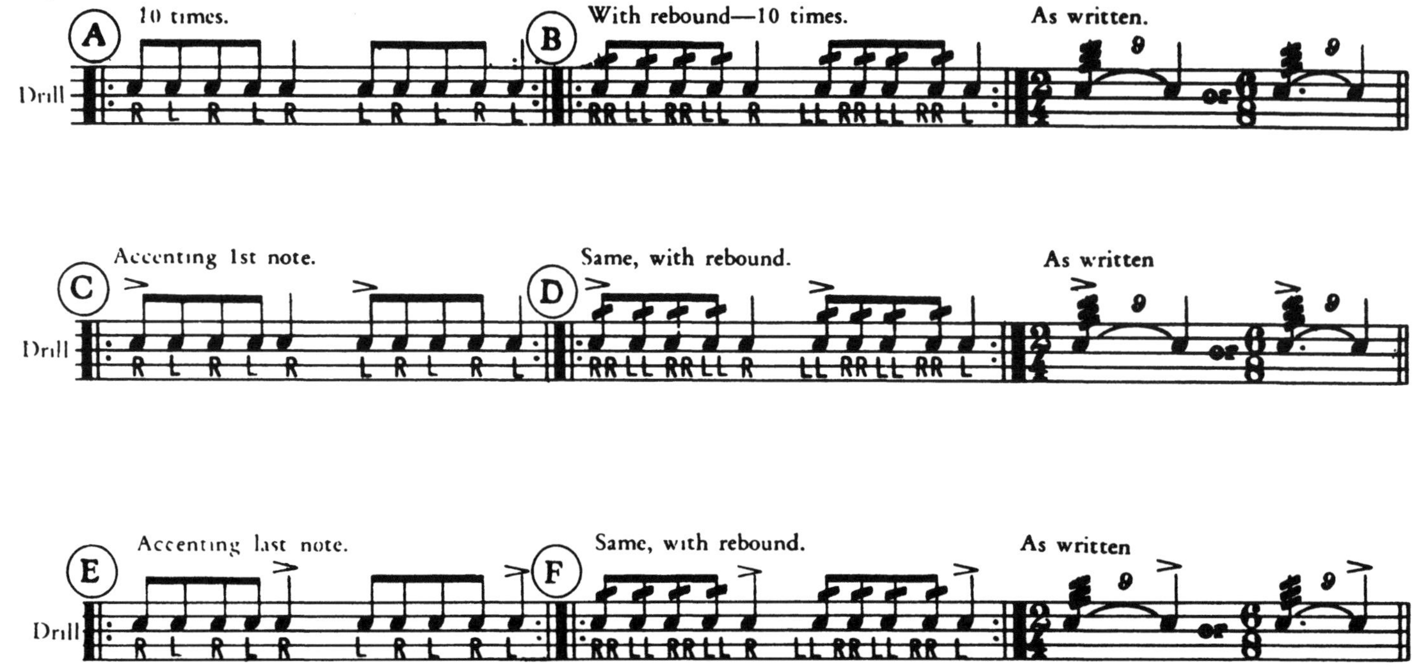

Note. Open and close 9 stroke rolls daily.

Excerpts from Marches

The following two-measure phrases were extracted from marches in well-known band folios. These phrases are used over and over in easy marches. Drill each phrase; each line; and the twenty phrases as a unit.

Two Four March Rhythms

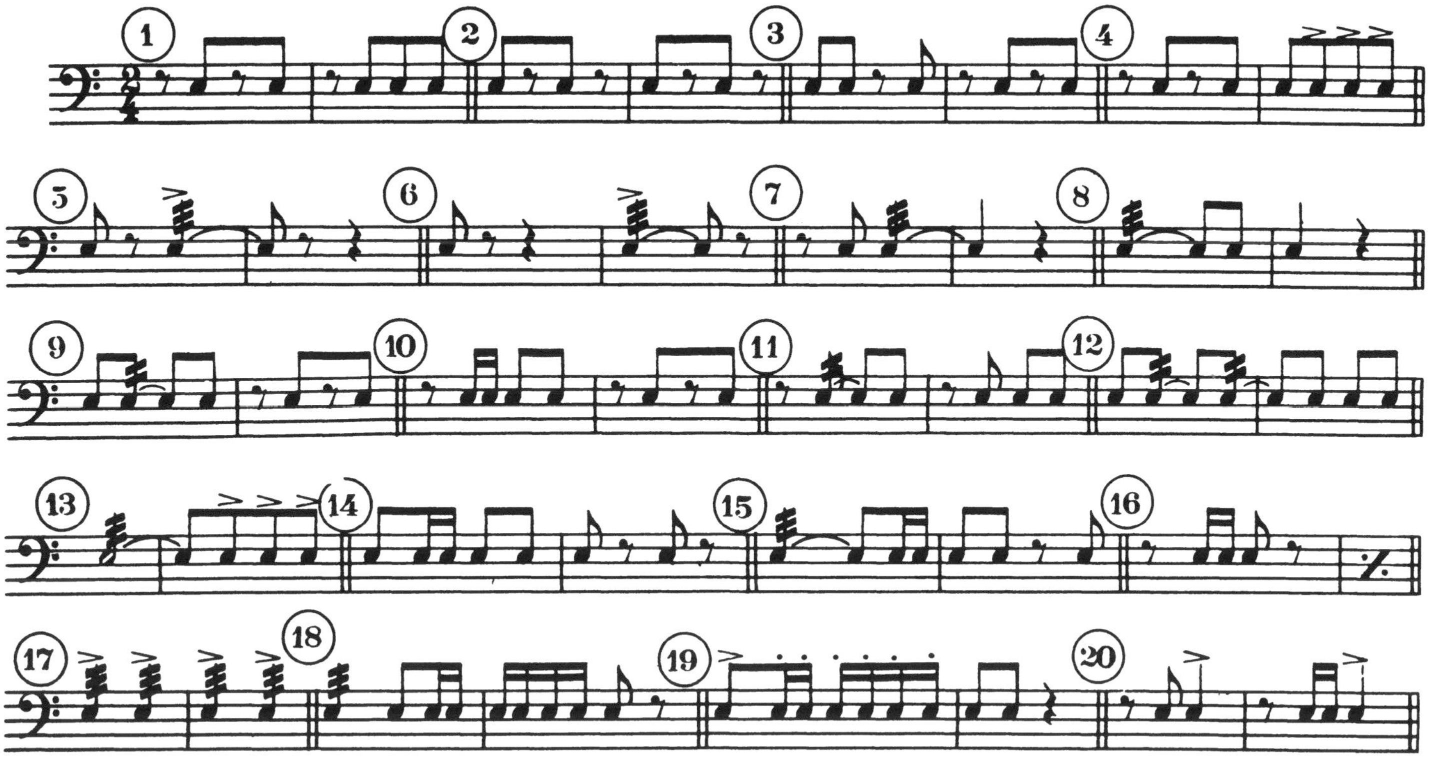

Six Eight March Rhythms

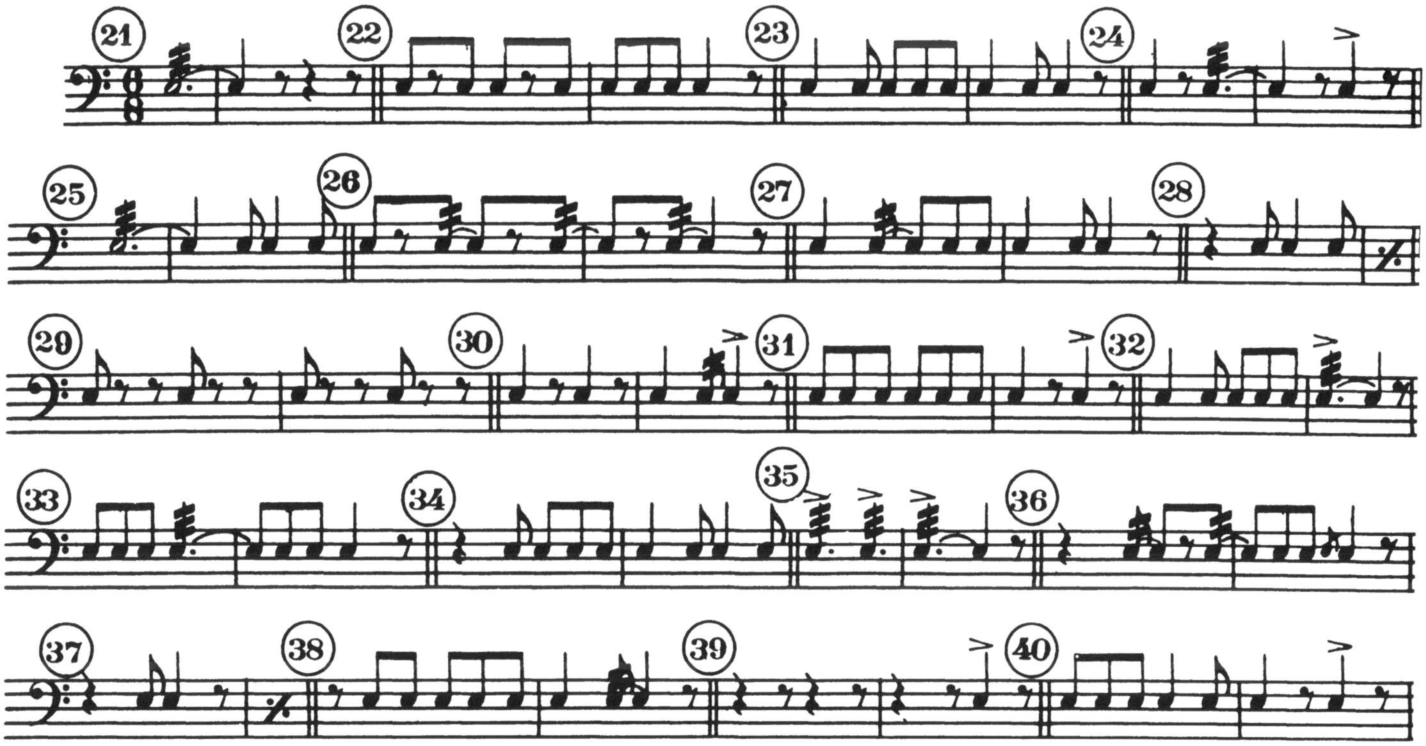

Review

After completing this book, the logical step is to Book Two of this series which continues with 46 additional "NEW" fundamentals.